CONSTITUTION

OF THE

Mercantile Library Association,

OF THE

CITY OF NEW YORK,

WITH THE

ACT OF INCORPORATION,

By-Laws and Regulations.

FOUNDED NOV. 9, 1820.

NEW YORK:
JORDAN, COMES & SEYMOUR, PRINTERS AND STATIONERS.
1870.

Presidents of the Association

FROM ITS ORGANIZATION.

1820-23..*LUCIUS BULL.*

1823-24..*CORNELIUS SAVAGE.*

1824-26..*BENJAMIN I. SEWARD.*

1827.31..*R. B. BROWN.*

1832-34..*JOHN W. STEBBINS.*

1834-35..*R. R. BOYD.*

1836-37..*CHARLES ROLFE.*

1838.....*EDMUND COFFIN.*

1839.....*JOHN S. WINTHROP.*

1839.....*ELIJAH WARD.*

1840.....*AUGUSTUS E. SILLIMAN.*

1841.....*HECTOR MORISON.*

1842.....*JOHN T. ROLLINS.*

1843.....*LEWIS McMULLEN.*

1843.....*RICHARD BURLEW.*

1844-45..*CHARLES E. MILNOR.*

1846-47..*CORNELIUS L EVERETT.*

1848.....*THOMAS W. GROSER.*

1849.....*ISAAC H. BAILEY.*

1850.....*THOMAS J. BAYAUD.*

1851.....*HENRY A. OAKLEY.*

1852.....*GEORGE PECKHAM.*

1853.....*WILLARD L. FELT.*

1854.....*DANIEL F. APPLETON.*

1855.....*D. REYNOLDS BUDD.*

1855-56..*GEORGE C. WOOD.*

1856.57..*JOHN CRERAR.*

1857-58..*ROWLAND H. TIMPSON.*

1857-58..*ALEXANDER P. FISKE.*

1858-59..*E. BOUDINOT SERVOSS.*

1859-60..*RICHARD A. BACHIA.*

1860-61..*CHAS.E.KING SHERMAN.*

1861-62..*CHARLES F. ALLEN.*

1862-63..*CHARLES OSGOOD.*

1863-64..*CHARLES H. SWORDS.*

1864-65..*THEODORE H. VULTEE.*

1865-66..*ROB'T. WALKER IRWIN.*

1866-67..*AARON C. ALLEN.*

1867-68..*ALEXANDER RHIND.*

1868-69..*CHARLES F. ALLEN.*

1869-70..*M. C. D. BORDEN.*

OFFICERS AND MEMBERS OF THE BOARD OF DIRECTION

AND

OFFICERS OF THE ASSOCIATION FOR 1870–71.

President,
M. C. D. BORDEN.

Vice-President,
W. T. PEOPLES.

Corresponding Secretary,
EDWARD HASLER.

Recording Secretary,
SAMUEL PUTNAM.

Treasurer,
GEORGE B. MILLS.

Directors of the First Class, to hold Office for One Year,
M. C. D. BORDEN,
EDWARD HASLER,
N. H. MYRICK,
GEO. B. MILLS.

Directors of the Second Class, to hold Office for Two Years,
W. T. PEOPLES,
SAMUEL PUTNAM,
A. W. SHERMAN,
J. C. CURRIE.

Directors of the Third Class, to hold Office for Three Years,
CHARLES F. ALLEN,
W. A. SHERMAN,
ASHER S. MILLS,
JNO. NICKINSON.

Librarian,
A. M. PALMER.

Assistant Librarian,
GEORGE COOPE.

MERCANTILE LIBRARY ASSOCIATION

STANDING COMMITTEES

OF THE

BOARD OF DIRECTION FOR 1870-'71.

Library.

WM, T. PEOPLES, *Chairman.* { CHAS. F. ALLEN, WM. A. SHERNAN.

Relations with Clinton Hall Association.

CHAS. F. ALLEN, *Chairman.* { ASHER S. MILLS, J. C. CURRIE.

Purchasing.

ASHER S. MILLS, *Chairman.* { JOHN NICKINSON, EDWARD HASLER.

Finance.

GEORGE B. MILLS, *Chairman.* { SAMUEL PUTNAM, WM. T. PEOPLES.

Auditing.

WM. A. SHERMAN, *Chairman.* { J. C. CURRIE, ASHER S. MILLS.

Lecture.

EDWARD HASLER, *Chairman.* { WM. A. SHERMAN, N. H. MYRICK.

Membership.

SAMUEL PUTNAM, *Chairman.* { WM. T. PEOPLES, CHAS. F. ALLEN.

Class.

J. C. CURRIE, *Chairman.* { A. W. SHERMAN. SAMUEL PUTNAM.

Catalogue.

JOHN NICKINSON, *Chairman.* { N. H. MYRICK, GEORGE B. MILLS.

Free Scholarships.

A. W. SHERMAN, *Chairman.* { EDWARD HASLER, JOHN NICKINSON.

Arrangements and Fine Arts.

N. H. MYRICK, *Chairman.* { GEORGE B. MILLS, A. W. SHERMAN.

ACT OF INCORPORATION.

AN ACT

To Incorporate "The Mercantile Library Association of the City of New York."

The People of the State of New York, represented in Senate and Assembly, do enact as follows:

SECTION 1. Robert Walker Irwin, Aaron C. Allen, Samuel B. Lyon, A. Judson Stone, James W. Edwards, Edwin P. Weed, Nathaniel D. White, Augustus T. Francis, George B. Emory, Albert H. Wheeler, George C. Lee, Jacob S. Isaacs, and such other persons as are now a corporation or association in the City of New York, called "The Mercantile Library Association of the City of New York," and such persons as shall hereafter become members of the corporation hereby created, are constituted a body corporate by the name of "The Mercantile Library Association of the City of New York," to be located in the City of New York for the promotion of useful knowledge.

SEC. 2. Said corporation shall have power to make and adopt a constitution, by-laws, rules and regulations for the admission, government, suspension and expulsion of its members, the collection of fees, fines and dues, the number, election and duties of its officers, the safe keeping and protection of its property and funds, and from time to time to alter, modify, change and repeal such constitution, by-laws, rules, and regulations. And in the meantime the present constitution, by-laws, rules and regulations shall be and continue in force, and the present officers and directors shall hold their respective offices until others are elected in their places.

Sec. 3. Said corporation shall have power to sue and may be sued by their corporate name, and shall have power to take by purchase, lease, gift, grant, devise and bequest, any real or personal estate, and hold, convey and transfer the same, provided they do not hold at any one time real property to the value of more than two hundred and fifty thousand dollars.

Sec. 4. Said corporation shall possess the general powers and be subject to the restrictions and liabilities prescribed in the third title of the eighteenth chapter, of the first part of the Revised Statutes.

Sec. 5. This act shall take effect immediately.

(Approved by the Governor, May 8, 1866.)

CONSTITUTION.

As Amended May 10th, 1870.

ARTICLE I.

OF MEMBERS.

SEC. 1. This Association shall be composed of three classes of members, viz: ACTIVE, SUBSCRIBING and HONORARY.

OF ACTIVE MEMBERS.

SEC. 2. Any person engaged on a salary as a clerk may become an Active Member of the Association, if approved by the Board of Direction, on subscribing to the Constitution, paying an initiation fee of $1,00, and $2,00 for the first six months. The regular dues of all active members hereafter, shall be $2,00, semi-annually, in advance.

Active members alone shall be entitled to vote and hold office.

SEC. 3. A membership of at least six months shall be requisite to make a member eligible to any office. A membership of at least three months shall be necessary to enable a member to vote at any election.

SEC. 4. If the dues of any member remain unpaid

for the term of twelve months, his rights of membership shall be forfeited, unless his delinquency be excused by the Board of Direction.

SEC. 5. Any person who shall be approved by the Board of Direction, may become a Subscribing Member of the Association, on the payment of ($5,00) five dollars, annually, or ($3,00) three dollars, semi-annually in advance, and shall be entitled to all the privileges of membership, except the right to vote and hold office.

SEC. 6. Persons of distinction may be elected Honorary Members of the Association by a vote of three-fourths of all the members of the Board of Direction, but no more than two persons shall be elected to such membership in any one year. Honorary members shall be entitled, for life, to the free use of the Library and Reading Room, and to all other privileges usually accorded to subscribing members.

ARTICLE II.

OF MEETINGS.

SEC. 1. There shall be an Annual Meeting of the members of the Association on the second Tuesday in May, for the purpose of receiving the report of the Board of Direction, and for the transaction of such other business as may be presented.

Fifty members shall constitute a quorum for the transaction of business.

SEC. 2. The President, at the request of the Board of Direction, or at the written request of one hundred members, stating the reason therefor, shall call a meeting of the Association for the transaction of special business; two weeks' public notice thereof having been given

ARTICLE III.

OF OFFICERS.

SEC. 1. The government of the Association shall be vested in a BOARD OF DIRECTION, which shall consist of TWELVE DIRECTORS, who shall be chosen to hold office for three years, except as hereinafter provided with reference to the Board first elected. Each member of this BOARD OF DIRECTION shall have one vote, excepting the President, who shall vote only in case of an equal division of the BOARD OF DIRECTION, and upon an election for HONORARY members.

SEC. 2. Immediately after the members of the BOARD OF DIRECTION, chosen at the first election under this Constitution, shall be assembled, they shall be divided by lot into three equal classes. The seats of the DIRECTORS of the first class shall be vacated at the end of the first year; of the second class at the end of the second year; of the third class at the end of the third year; so that one-third may be chosen every year.

SEC. 3. Any vacancy in the Board of Direction occasioned by resignation or otherwise, shall be filled for the unexpired time by the Board, a plurality of votes constituting a choice.

Sec. 4. There shall be an Annual Election to fill the seats of the outgoing Directors on the Tuesday succeeding the Annual Meeting, the polls to open at 8 o'clock A. M., and to close at 9 o'clock P. M. Such election shall be by ballot. No member shall be entitled to vote who is in arrears for dues.

Sec. 5. At least two weeks previous to each Annual Election, the Board of Direction shall give public notice thereof, and shall also appoint a Board of Inspectors to superintend such election and if any of the Inspectors shall fail to attend at the time appointed for the election those who do attend may fill the vacancy. If one or more of the requisite number of Directors balloted for at any such election shall, for any cause fail to be elected the Board of Inspectors shall order a new election to be held within one week thereafter to fill the place or places of those so failing to be elected.

Sec. 6. The Directors chosen at each election shall take their seats on the Tuesday next succeeding their election.

Sec. 7. The Officers of the Board of Direction shall be a President, Vice-President, Corresponding Secretary, Recording Secretary and Treasurer, They shall be elected by and from the Board of Direction to hold office for one year.

Sec. 8. The Officers of the Board of Direction shall be Officers of the Association.

Sec. 9. The President shall preside at all meetings of the Board of Direction and of the Association; preserve order therein, and in case of an equal division on any question, give the casting vote. He shall, with the Treasurer, sign all checks of the Association for the disbursement of funds.

SEC. 10. THE VICE-PRESIDENT, in the absence of the PRESIDENT, shall perform all the duties of that officer.

SEC. 11. The CORRESPONDING SECRETARY shall conduct the correspondence of the Association, under the superintendence of the Board of Direction.

SEC. 12. The RECORDING SECRETARY shall keep an accurate record of the transactions of the Association and of the Board of Direction.

SEC. 13. The TREASURER shall, subject to the approval of the Board of Direction, have charge and custody of all the securities of the Association, collect the principal of the same as they become due, collect the dividends or interest on investments as they mature, and shall deposit to the credit of "THE MERCANTILE LIBRARY ASSOCIATION," without delay, all funds received by him for or on account of the Association, in such BANK or INSTITUTION as may have been designated by the Board of Direction. He shall, with the President, sign all checks, and keep a regular account of the finances of the Association, an abstract of which shall be presented at each ANNUAL MEETING, with the ANNUAL REPORT of the Board of Direction. He shall give security in the sum of FIVE THOUSAND DOLLARS for the faithful discharge of his trust.

SEC. 14. The moneys of the Association shall be disbursed only by checks upon the INSTITUTION holding the same, signed by the PRESIDENT and TREASURER.

SEC. 15. The Board of Direction shall have full

power to appropriate funds, enact By-laws for its own government, and for the government of the Association; make all proper provisions and regulations for the preservation, management and direction of the LIBRARY, READING ROOM and CABINET, and to conduct the affairs of the Association. The Board shall meet at least once a month, for the transaction of business and at each ANNUAL MEETING shall report its proceedings for the preceding year.

SEC. 16. No member of the Board of Direction shall receive, directly or indirectly, any compensation for the services he shall, in his official capacity, render the Association.

SEC. 17. The Board of Direction shall have power to establish BRANCH LIBRARIES in such localities, and upon such conditions, as it may deem just and proper; provided that no member shall have the right to use BRANCH LIBRARIES established beyond the limits of the CITY OF NEW YORK, who does not pay at least $5,00 annual dues and that no person subscribing to the Association through such outside BRANCH LIBRARIES shall have the right to vote or hold office.

SEC. 18. In case of flagrant official or personal misconduct, the Board of Direction shall have power, by a vote of three-fourths of its whole number, to expel a member of the Board—two weeks' previous notice of the charges against him having been rendered in writing to the PRESIDENT, who shall thereupon and within one week thereafter, furnish a copy of such charges to the member against whom they are made; and in case of flagrant misconduct on the part of any member of the Association, the Board of Direction shall have the power of suspending said member by a vote of three-fourths of its whole number—two weeks' previous notice of the charges having been given him by the Corresponding Secretary, in writing, served upon him personally or mailed to his last address as shall appear upon the books of the Association—but he shall have the right to appeal to the succeeding Annual Meeting, for its decision as to his restoration or expulsion.

SEC. 19. It shall be the duty of the Board of Direction to appoint a Librarian, with such assistants as may be deemed necessary, and to require of him good and sufficient surety in a sum not less than five thousand dollars, ($5,000), for the faithful discharge of his duties.

SEC. 20. A Committee shall be appointed each year, by the Board of Direction, to examine the books and other property of the Association, and report thereon, at least one month previous to each Annual Meeting.

ARTICLE IV.

OF DONATIONS AND BEQUESTS.

SEC. 1. In case any moneys shall accrue to the Association by gifts or demise (without condition as to the mode in which such donation shall be expended), it shall be the duty of the Board of Direction to fund the moneys thus acquired in such securities as shall be approved of by two-thirds of its whole number, and the custodian of said moneys or securities, shall give bonds for the safe keeping of the same, (in such amount as may be fixed upon by the Board of Direction); and no part of the principal of such funds shall be expended for any purpose whatever, without the previous sanction of two-thirds of the members present at a Special or Annual Meeting of the Association.

ARTICLE V.

OF AMENDMENTS.

SEC. 1. There shall be no alteration of this Constitution, unless the same shall have been proposed to the Board of Direction at least one month previous to an Annual Meeting, and then approved by two-thirds of the members of the Association present at such meeting.

SEC. 2. This Constitution shall take effect immediately.

BY-LAWS AND REGULATIONS.

Article 1. The Library shall be open from 8 o'clock, A. M., until 9 o'clock, P. M.; and the Reading-Room from 8 o'clock, A. M., until 10 o'clock, P. M., every day—except Sundays, legal holidays, and such other days as the Board of Direction may designate.

Art. 2. The Librarian shall keep a full and accurate catalogue of all the books, magazines, maps, charts, newspapers, and works of art belonging to the Association, and arrange them in proper order; he shall keep a duplicate of the same, which shall at all times be open to the inspection of the members. He shall make a record of all books, maps, charts, &c., presented to the Association, in a book provided for that purpose, with the names of the donors.

Art. 3. He shall register, in ledgers prepared for that purpose, and to be kept in the Library-room, the name of every member of the Association, and shall in no case deliver a book to any member until the name and address of such member is registered; he shall preserve an accurate account of the number of every volume delivered by him, the name of the person to whom delivered, the time of taking and returning the same, together with the forfeiture arising from every default.

ART. 4. He shall collect all dues and forfeitures incurred by the members, and account for the same to the Treasurer at the close of each month, or oftener if required by the Board of Direction.

ART. 5. He shall, when required, report to the Board of Direction the names of such members as may refuse to pay their forfeitures, or lose or damage any book belonging to the Library; and the names of all delinquents, with the amount of dues remaining unpaid.

ART. 6. He shall suffer no person, except members of the Board, to remove a book from its place in the Library without his permission; nor shall he allow any but Directors and Ex-Directors to frequent the alcoves or space within the enclosure, unless to consult books of reference.

ART. 7. He shall see that the books, Library-room and Reading-rooms, are kept in good order; shall duly observe the instructions which may be given him by the Board of Direction, and take care that the regulations relative to the loaning of books be strictly adhered to.

ART. 8. Books shall be delivered to members of the Association when called for by cards prepared for that purpose, properly filled and signed by the member himself, or by some one authorized to draw for him.

ART. 9. Every member shall be entitled to have out one work at a time not exceeding three volumes; but any member desiring to draw another work, already having one out, may do so by paying at the rate of ten cents for each week or part of a week that it shall be retained.

ART. 10. Members may retain each work the length of time specified on the covers on the books. They shall be fined ten cents for each week, or part of a week, that a book shall have been detained beyond the time so prescribed.

ART. 11. Any member may open a duplicate account for his own use by paying one dollar half yearly in advance.

ART. 12. The Librarian shall ascertain at the close of each month, or oftener, what books have been kept over the time allowed, and shall send notice to members in default, requesting the immediate return of their books.

ART. 13. If any member lose, or deface with marginal notes, or by marking, or otherwise injure a book, he shall make the same good to the Librarian ; and if the book lost or injured be one of a set, he shall pay the Librarian for the use of the Association, the full value of said set, and may thereupon receive the remaining volumes as his property.

ART. 14. No member shall be permitted to receive a book from the Library until he shall have paid all sums due from him to the Association, and made good all damages and losses which he may have occasioned.

ART. 15. The books marked in the catalogue as books of reference, thus (*), and such others as may from time to time be specially designated by the Board, shall not be taken from the Library, except by special permission of a member of the Board of Direction.

Art. 16. Any member wishing to withdraw from the Association, must inform the Librarian of it, see that his resignation be registered, and pay up his dues and fees, else he will be considered as continuing a member, and charged accordingly—unless otherwise ordered by the Board of Direction.

Art. 17. No book shall be reserved by the Librarian for any Director or member.

Regulations of the Reading-Room.

ARTICLE 1. The Reading-room shall be under the SUPERVISION OF THE SUPERINTENDENT, who shall take charge of, and keep in their places, all the books, periodicals, and newspapers kept therein. It shall be his or her duty to supply the occupants of the room with such books from the LIBRARY as they may wish to consult; and to enforce such rules and regulations for the government of this department as the Board may enact.

ART. 2. Blank forms will be furnished by the SUPERINTENDENT to those who desire to consult works from the Library, in which the applicant shall fill in the title of the work and date of application, and affix his signature and number of the folio thereto, or number of his card of admission, if a visitor, when he shall obtain the book with but little delay; and such applicant will be held responsible for it until the redemption of the written application by the return of the work.

ART. 3. None but MEMBERS will be allowed the privileges of the READING-ROOM, unless introduced by a member of the Association; and members shall exhibit their tickets of subscription when required to do so by the Superintendent; and no member will be allowed the use of the READING-ROOM unless all dues and forfeitures are liquidated.

ART. 4. Any member may have the privilege of introducing a friend who is a non-resident, whose name shall be registered by the Librarian in a book provided for that purpose, and who will receive a card of admission to the Reading-Room for the term of four weeks; persons so introduced may consult books in the Reading-Room and Library, but shall not be privileged to take them out of the rooms of the Association.

ART. 5. Any member who shall mutilate the periodicals or papers placed in the Reading-Room, or remove them therefrom, shall be liable to a fine equal to four times the cost thereof.

ART. 6. No periodical work shall be taken from the room until two months shall have elapsed from the time of its being received.

ART. 7. No *conversation* will be allowed in the Reading-room otherwise than in a whisper.

ART. 8. *No member shall be permitted to sit in the Reading-Room with his hat on, nor will smoking be allowed in any of the rooms of the Association.*

ARTICLES OF AGREEMENT

BETWEEN

THE CLINTON HALL ASSOCIATION,

OF THE CITY OF NEW YORK,

AND THE

MERCANTILE LIBRARY ASSOCIATION,

Of the City of New York.

THIS agreement between the "Clinton Hall Association of the City of New York," of the first part, and "The Mercantile Library Association of the City of New York," of the second part,

Witnesseth, That whereas the Clinton Hall Association, in view of their original plan and articles of subscription, for the better attainment of the objects for which the said Association was established, have sold the building called Clinton Hall, at the south-west corner of Nassau and Beekman Streets, and have purchased the premises known as the Opera House, situated at the intersection of Astor Place and Eighth Street, and are altering, arranging, and fitting up the same, according to their plans now adopted, they do hereby stipulate and agree with the Mercantile Library Association, as follows:

1. That the party of the second part may occupy, free of rent, two rooms in said building, designated on said plans of the Library and Reading-Room, for those purposes ; also four apartments, to be set apart hereafter, by the party of the first part, for class-rooms (if required) and other purposes, in accordance with the objects of the Mercantile Library Association ; and may also use the Lecture Hall for general meetings of the Association, and for lectures to be delivered to its members as often as twice in each week ; which privileges shall be enjoyed under such terms and conditions as are hereinafter expressed, and for so long a time as they are fulfilled to the satisfaction of the party of the first part. Additional room for the Library and Reading-room, and additional nights for the use of the Lecture Hall, shall be set apart, if necessary, upon the same condition.

2. That when the cost of altering, arranging, and fitting up said premises at the intersection of Astor Place and Eighth Street, and the cost of the site, with the accruing interest shall have been paid, either by new subscriptions, by the rents of the building, or from any other source, the funds arising from rents shall be laid out in such books, cabinets, or scientific apparatus, as the party of the first part may deem proper ; the said party reserving to itself the right to make earlier appropriations for these purposes. All such books, cabinets, or apparatus, shall continue to belong to the party of the first part, and shall be deposited in the building, and be used by the members of the Clinton Hall and Mercantile Library Associations, under such regulations as may be made by the party of the first part for that purpose.

And the party of the second part doth hereby stipulate and agree with the party of the first part, as follows :

1. That its Library shall be deposited in the room, or rooms of said building appropriated to receive it ; that the room or rooms set apart as Reading-rooms shall be used by the members for that purpose ; and that the Lecture Hall shall be used for the general meetings of the Association, and for the lectures which are delivered to its members.

2. That during the continuance of the agreement, it will pay the taxes on said building, if any are imposed ; and will, at its own cost, keep the rooms it occupies in full and complete repair, and defray such proportion of the expenses of lighting and warming the house as may be fair and equitable.

3. That the whole income of the party of the second part, after defraying the necessary charges of the establishment, (not including the expenses of lectures), shall be annually invested in books, which shall be deposited in the Library, with its other books: and the shareholders of the Clinton Hall Association shall have access to the Library, free of charge, under the same regulations as the members of the Mercantile Library are subjected to, without giving to such shareholders a right to vote in the elections of that Association.

4. That in case the Trustees of the Clinton Hall Association shall be of opinion that the party of the second part shall convert the rooms it occupies in the said building to any purpose not intended by the

party of the first part; or that the character of the Mercantile Library Association shall have become so changed that its usefulness shall have ceased; or that it shall have deposited immoral or irreligious books in its Library, and not removed them within twenty days after being advised to do so by the *Trustees of the Clinton Hall Association;* or that they shall have wilfully neglected or violated any of the stipulations contained in this agreement,—then the said Trustees may call a meeting of the Shareholders of the Clinton Hall Association and the Directors of the Mercantile Library Association, and lay before the meeting the facts to show that either of these contingencies has occurred; and the Shareholders of the Clinton Hall Association, after a full consideration, may determine to resume the use and occupation of the rooms so appropriated, and the books, cabinets, and apparatus, purchased by the party of the first part; and such determination shall be final and conclusive on the party of the second part, who shall thereupon surrender and give up the premises, and the said books, cabinets, and apparatus, to the party of the first part, and shall remove from said building after thirty days' notice of such determination.

5. That the Shareholders of the Clinton Hall Association may attend the course of lectures which may be delivered to the Mercantile Library Association, on the same terms as are enjoyed by its members.

In witness whereof, the said parties have respectively caused their corporate seals to be hereunto affixed, and these presents to be signed by their respective Presidents the third day of November, one thousand eight hundred and fifty-three.

THE CLINTON HALL ASSOCIATION,

By *Wilson G. Hunt*, President. [L. S.]

THE MERCANTILE LIBRARY ASSOCIATION OF THE CITY OF NEW YORK,

By *Willard L. Felt*, President. [L. S.]

PERMANENT CATALOGUE FUND.

The President and Corresponding Secretary of the Mercantile Library Association, and the President of the Clinton Hall Association, *ex officio*, and two members of the Library, not officers, shall be the Trustees of said Fund. They shall be known as the Trustees of the "Permanent Catalogue Fund," and shall have power to supply any vacancy which may occur in their body until the next annual meeting of this Association, when a new Trustee shall be chosen. They shall also have power to appoint their own officers, and to make such by-laws and rules as may be necessary for their own regulation, and shall present an annual report to the Board of Directors at least one week before the Annual Meeting.

It shall be the duty of said Trustees to invest the principal and accumulations of said Fund in such securities as they may approve, and to deposit all moneys belonging to said Fund, not thus invested, in whatever Savings Bank they may appoint.

The Trustees shall, at the request of the Board of Directors, pay to them, from year to year, the income of the Fund ; said income to be expended under the direction of the Board to prepare a catalogue of the books of the Associations, and for no other purpose.

Whenever, from time, to time it may be deemed expedient to print any catalogues that may have been prepared as above, the Trustees shall advance to the Board of Directors the amount necessary ; said Trustees to be reimbursed by the proceeds of the sale of all Catalogues thus printed. and by moneys taken from the funds of the Association, sufficient to make the total reimbursement to the Trustees each year at least fifteen (15) per cent. on the amount they may have advanced from the principal of the fund.

WILSON G. HUNT, Pres. of Clinton Hall Ass'n.

M. C. D. BORDEN, " Mer. Library "

EDWARD HASLER, Cor. Sec. " "

Ex-Officio Trustees.

DANIEL F. APPLETON, chosen at Ann. Meeting.

WILLARD L. FELT, " " "

Trustees.

www.ingramcontent.com/pod-product-compliance
Lightning Source LLC
LaVergne TN
LVHW011141110826
845150LV00008B/2442

* 9 7 8 1 4 1 8 1 9 3 2 0 1 *